THE SOUND OF KWANZAA

By Dimitrea Tokunbo   Illustrated by Lisa Cohen

SCHOLASTIC PRESS
NEW YORK

Acknowledgments

The author would like to give a special thanks to Robin Holme
and David Wright for introducing her to the cookbook
Raw Food Made Easy For 1 or 2 People by Jennifer Cornbleet,
which inspired the recipe for my No-Cook Kwanzaa Brownie Bites.

Library of Congress Cataloging-in-Publication Data

Tokunbo, Dimitrea.
The sound of Kwanzaa / Dimitrea Tokunbo ; illustrated by Lisa Cohen. 1st ed.
p. cm.
Includes bibliographical references.
ISBN-13: 978-0-545-01865-4
ISBN-10: 0-545-01865-X
1. Kwanzaa—Juvenile literature. 2. African Americans—Social life and customs—Juvenile literature.
I. Cohen, Lisa, 1963- ill. II. Title.

GT4403.T65 2008
394.2612dc22

2007025916

Printed in Singapore 46

10 9 8 7 6 5 4 3   10 11 12 13
First edition, October 2009
The text type was set in Blockhead unplugged.
Book design by Susan Schultz

For Andrea, Brian, Chloe, and Dobbin —D.T.

For Mischa, Jackson, Teylor, Austyn, Hannah, Phillip,
and Hannah Barnes: Shine a light of love! —L.C.

Come close, gather 'round.

Listen to the sound of Kwanzaa.

Loving words and greeting family,

we stand together for UMOJA.

UMOJA means "unity."

One black candle gently shines

to welcome our first Kwanzaa night.

Come close, gather 'round.
Listen to the sound of Kwanzaa.
Working hands and ancient stories,
we learn our traditions for KUJICHAGULIA.
KUJICHAGULIA means "self-determination."
One red candle gently flickers
to honor our second Kwanzaa night.

Come close, gather 'round.
Listen to the sound of Kwanzaa.
Banging hammers and sweeping brooms,
we share the chores for UJIMA.
UJIMA means "collective work and
responsibility."
One green candle gently shimmers
to lighten our third Kwanzaa night.

Come close, gather 'round. Listen to the sound of Kwanzaa. Laughing shoppers and chanting merchants, we support our neighborhoods for UJAMAA. UJAMAA means "cooperative economics."

Another red candle gently twinkles to brighten our fourth Kwanzaa night.

Come close, gather 'round.
Listen to the sound of Kwanzaa.
Sharing dreams and setting goals,
we plan our future for NIA.
NIA means "purpose."
Another green candle gently glows
to illuminate our fifth Kwanzaa night.

Come close, gather 'round.

Listen to the sound of Kwanzaa.

Beating drums and singing voices,

we perform for KUUMBA.

KUUMBA means "creativity."

Another red candle gently burns

to warm our sixth Kwanzaa night.

Come close, gather 'round.
Listen to the sound of Kwanzaa.
Thankful prayers and loud *Harambees*,
we celebrate our lives for IMANI.
IMANI means "faith."
The last green candle gently sparkles
to bless our seventh Kwanzaa night.

Harambee!
Harambee!
Harambee!

AUTHOR'S NOTE

When I was much younger, my father took me to Harlem. We stopped to visit one of his friends. As my father introduced us, his voice boomed, "This is the man who created Kwanzaa!"

It was true. Dr. Maulana Karenga started this African American celebration in 1966. He named it after the Swahili word *kwanza*, which means "first fruits." Kwanzaa is observed for seven days from December 26 to January 1.

Kwanzaa is a time to reaffirm African American culture by practicing the Nguzo Saba (seven guiding principles), which are:

1. UMOJA (oo-MO-jah) unity
2. KUJICHAGULIA (koo-jee-chah-GOO-lee-ah) self-determination
3. UJIMA (oo-JEE-mah) collective work and responsibility
4. UJAMAA (oo-jah-MAH-ah) cooperative economics
5. NIA (NEE-ah) purpose
6. KUUMBA (koo-OOM-bah) creativity
7. IMANI (ee-MAH-nee) faith

Each day, the question is asked, "Habari gani?" which means "What's the news?"

The response is to say the Nguzo Saba for that day and to light a candle on the Kinara (candleholder). Another Swahili word I mention in this book is *harambee*, an exclamation that means "let's pull together."

On the last day of Kwanzaa, many African American families have a karamu (feast or party). When my daughters and I were invited to our first Karamu, we wanted to bring one of our favorite desserts, brownies, but we wanted to give them a special festive twist in honor of the celebration.

We decided to individually wrap bite-size pieces of brownie and a small slip of paper, each having one of the Nguzo Saba written on it.

Toward the end of the party, our hosts passed around the dish with our gift-wrapped brownies to the guests. One by one, we all took a brownie, unwrapped it, and shared how we planned to use the principle we found during the upcoming year.

Here is one of my family's favorite recipes. We call it "No-Cook Kwanzaa Brownie Bites." You can make and share them at your next Karamu. Even though these brownies require no cooking, adult supervision is suggested when preparing them.

ENJOY! —D.T.

NO-COOK KWANZAA bROWNiE biteS

Ingredients
1/2 cup walnuts
1/2 cup almonds
1/2 cup pecans
Pinch of salt
Pinch of cinnamon
3 tablespoons cocoa powder, unsweetened
3 teaspoons maple syrup
1/4 teaspoon vanilla extract
12 to 14 large dates, pitted
Vegetable oil
1/2 cup confectioners' sugar
(or you can use cocoa powder or almond meal)

Equipment
Measuring cups and spoons
Food processor
Mixing bowl
Plastic sandwich bag

What You Do

1. With a grown-up's help, place walnuts, almonds, and
pecans into food processor and pulse until finely chopped.

2. Sprinkle your pinch of salt, pinch of cinnamon,
and unsweetened cocoa powder
evenly over nut mixture and pulse until mixed.

3. Pour the maple syrup and vanilla extract evenly over mixture.
Add dates and pulse until evenly mixed.

4. Rub hands with a little vegetable oil and dump brownie mixture
out of food processor and into a mixing bowl.

5. Pinch about thumb-size pieces of brownie mixture
and press into squares or roll into balls.

6. Dust brownie bites in confectioners' sugar by
gently shaking in sugar-filled sandwich bag.

Makes about three dozen No-Cook Kwanzaa Brownie Bites.

bibliography

Davis Pinkney, Andrea. *Seven Candles for Kwanzaa*. New York: Dial Books for Young Readers, a Division of Penguin Books USA Inc., 1993.

Karenga, Maulana. *The African American Holiday of Kwanzaa: A Celebration of Family, Community and Culture*. Los Angeles: University of Sankore Press, 1989.

Meachen Rau, Dana. *Kwanzaa: A True Book*. New York: Children's Press, a Division of Grolier Publishing Co., Inc., 2000.

Morninghouse, Sundaira. *Habar Gani?* North Carolina: Open Hand Publishing, LLC, 1992.

Shelf Medearis, Angela. *The Seven Days of Kwanzaa*. New York: Scholastic Inc., 1994.